MAD ABOUT THE DOG

MAD ABOUT THE DOG

Belinda Harley

Souvenir Press

First published in Great Britain in 2009 by Souvenir Press Ltd
43 Great Russell Street, London WC1B 3PD

ISBN 9780285638631

Typeset by M Rules
Printed and bound in Great Britain by
CPI Antony Rowe, Chippenham, Wiltshire

Goofy would wish me to thank four vets: Dino Bourlogiannis in Corfu; Keith Butt; Richard Allport; and Clive Elwood; to whose remarkable skill and compassion he owed his life. This book is dedicated to my beloved friend Spiros Anemogiannis, who loved him too.

CHAPTER 1

All over dog

Nothing moved on the terrace in the afternoon sun, except the quick flick of lizards in the rough dry stone walls. Suddenly, there was a frantic scrabbling from behind the wall itself. A black nose and a ginger and white face appeared, followed by the rest of a small dog, who made a giant leap for me.

As my friend Daphne said, "Dog looked at Belinda. Belinda looked at Dog. *And it was all over.*"

I have always loved Paxos. It has the lush green calm that Corfu, in the days when it flaunted its beauty at the writer Lawrence Durrell, once had. I had always liked the way that, when they made small-scale maps of the Ionian Sea, they didn't bother to put Paxos, let alone its tiny sibling Anti-Paxos, on the map at all. They were just left to the imagination . . . As a child, arriving by caique, I was bewitched by it; as an adult, when tired and saddened by the pressures of the outside world, I used it as a place where mentally one could detox from London, as far from the canapé circuit as it is possible to get. I would take long walks – christened "death marches" by my friend Daphne, who often came to stay – when I rented a small house in the hills. Armed with a water bottle and a straw hat that would have shamed a seaside donkey, I would climb steep paths through the olive groves, exhilarated. Every sense was awakened: I'd catch a sudden intense whiff of fresh figs, oozing their perfume over a sunny wall; shiver, after climbing a hill in the hot sun, at the extraordinary transition into the deep dark cool of the porch of a lonely church, shockingly white amid the olive trees. I loved it. Of course I was just a visitor; but I knew by sight the mothers, fathers, children, aunts, uncles, grandparents, and cousins of almost everyone in the tiny village of Loggos.

Up in the hills, the small stone house that had belonged to Spiro's mother Electra baked like a golden bun in the sun, among crumbling terraces of olives and almond trees. It was one of those hot afternoons on Paxos when the only thing to do . . . is absolutely nothing. Everything was mesmerised by the heat, the stillness burst only by the tantrum of crickets. We would wait for evening before moving again, when a cool breeze would lift the air and the Paxiots – who are inveterate nocturnal animals, young and old – would suddenly emerge down in the village beside the sea, talking on the jetty walls, drinking, eating, sniffing the scent of jasmine mingled with their last cigarette in the night air. They prepared for this tremendous burst of night-time activity with a short but very sweet sleep; we followed their example, drowsing in the hot afternoon without a thought of inter-ruption.

Having hurled himself into my arms, this refugee dog was going nowhere. He was – debatably – spaniel, with a beautiful head and dark intelligent eyes. His stocky body and broad white chest seemed to justify legs rather longer than those God had given him. God had also made him ginger, over his ears and in patches elsewhere. The proud body and slightly stubby little legs gave him an endearing and entirely original shape. He licked me confidently.

I rang my friend Spiro, who had rented me the house for the summer. "Oh, that is Goofy! He runs away from his owners up the hill. Belinda, that is a wonderful dog – he came to stay with me in the winter." I wasn't sure that the name Goofy suited him at all; he was too sussed out, too bright. But then I remembered that my Greek neighbours sometimes adopted English or American showbusiness or sports celebrity names for their dogs; there was a poodle-shaped animal at the village shop who answered, bizarrely, to the name of Alan, after an unwit-ting Alan Shearer.

As the evening cool came, I walked down the dappled

stone track through the olive groves to the village by the sea, my new companion running delightedly in small circles round me. I expected that on arrival in the village, Goofy would be off, prospecting for food from holiday-makers at the tiny tables by the water. I was secretly rather flattered at his loyalty. He would head off towards each café table and cajole food, focussing pleading eyes on the most tender-hearted target. Then he would run back to me. Never was a dog so gregarious; but he was also touchingly faithful.

Goofy's attachment made me feel a little awkward; I knew he had a home to go to. Spiro assured me that it wasn't a problem, as his owners worked from early in the morning until very late at night, and kept Goofy tied up on a short chain. He said the dog wasn't at all keen on this: whenever it was possible, Goofy made his escape.

Night wore on, and Daphne and I had to drive in my little car to the port of Gaios, where a friend had arrived. Farewell Goofy . . . but in a single bound, he jumped onto the back seat of the car, front paws squarely placed so that he could lean out of the window as we drove, as proud as the figurehead on the prow of a ship. As his ears flew back in the wind, it looked as if he were smiling . . . I gave myself a shake.

When we tumbled out in the port, I became concerned. Would I be responsible for the dog becoming lost, so far from home? But Goofy stayed proprietorially by my side, as we picked up my friend Laura and brought her back to our village for drinks and dinner. When we drove her back that night and returned to my house, Goofy was still on board. Daphne, attempting to forestall what she saw as a disaster, suddenly announced "The dog needs to get out here". There was the track which led to the painted gate, which led to the house where Goofy was kept chained up . . . Firmly, she placed Goofy on the path to his home, slammed the car door, and instructed me to drive. "What a terribly nice dog", I said. "Stop it", she said.

She could have saved herself the trouble. Two hours later, padding barefoot into the kitchen for a glass of water, she found two eyes glowing amber in the dark with entreaty. Without waking me, she locked the dog outside. He would have to go home. But when I woke in the morning, and threw open the doors from my bedroom onto the terrace, there, having curled up for the whole night outside my room, was Goofy.

Goofy would have been the despair of pedigree breeders. He had his good points: his coat was white with patches of burnished copper, like splashes of cinnamon, distributed over his ears and body with the casual artistry and assurance of an abstract painter. He could have been what they call a Britanny spaniel; perhaps a mixture of Cocker and Springer; but the little lamb-chop legs had led to one of the villagers naming him Stumpy.

Goofy might have been short in the leg department, but he was very long on wits. Intelligence positively shone from him. He approached humans on equal terms, fixing his eyes on theirs. One foreleg was already thinner than the others, and wasted, and gave him a lolloping gait that was the price, I later discovered, of ill treatment. I was deeply impressed that he never allowed this to interfere with his willingness to know people, and if he could, trust them.

Imagine you were appointed teacher to a class of small boys, and discovered that fully one in three of them was called by the same name. Despite the rich opportunities for confusion (*Spiro, have you seen Spiro? Yes, he and Spiro went to Spiro's friend Spiro's house . . .*) boys are called after the patron saint of Corfu, St Spiridon; and since Christian names are passed down families, there will be no escaping Spiros on the islands till the end of time.

But for me, there was only one Spiro. He was not a boyfriend; yet as Goofy was to teach me, deep instinctive sympathies can exist between beings of very different breeds. I had been visiting the village for several years before I got to know him. I would see him arriving mid-morning on a battered Vespa he had painted the colour of deep red wine, dark circles under his eyes from a string of late nights, long dark corkscrew curls tied behind his neck. The tiny jetty of Loggos stretched like a white finger into the sea; on it, the old customs house had become the *Taxidi*. Tables and chairs faced the sea on both sides, so that you could dangle your toes in the water as you looked at the tiny harbour on one side, or scanned the channel for elusive glimpses of dolphins on the other. Spiro had filled it with his own idiosyncratic character and personality; I, who fancied I knew a bit about the subject, thought it the most simply beautiful bar in the world.

Spiro decorated the bar with sheaves of wild arum lilies, and filled fishermen's panniers with huge watermelons, to make cocktails with iced vodka; he played the accordion with friends on the mandolin and bouzouki; he discussed literature from Plato to Marquez; he was kind, passionate and impulsive. He did not suffer fools gladly; one morning as we sat over coffees, a philandering middle-aged Englishman came over to tell us all about himself. "I've just heard my girlfriend is on the ferry on her way here, and my wife is still on the island!" he said. "Now *that* will be interesting . . ." "No, it won't", said Spiro.

Best of all, on lost afternoons, I would sit behind him on the Vespa and we would bump along tracks I didn't know existed, to deserted villages that had crumbled into ruins. Here we would explore, collecting old bottles and ceramics that would be cleaned and would reappear in the bar; when I next returned to Paxos, there they would be; signs that I belonged.

It was because of Spiro that I had rented the little house in the olive groves; it was because of Spiro that I was in the right place to be found, one hot afternoon, by a dog on the run.

Many times I had puffed up the hill to the tiny hamlet

in the olive groves, high above the sea, and seen the painted garden gate to the house where I now knew that Goofy lived. Spiro explained that Goofy's owners could not look after him during the day, or even the evening, so he was chained up for interminable periods. Spiro wasn't keen on my being alone in the hills; entirely unsubstantiated stories circulated about the danger from refugee Albanians. He suggested that we offered to Goofy's owners to look after him while I was in Greece. The owner shrugged his acceptance, and Goofy – I thought temporarily – was mine.

My funny little timeshare dog and I became a familiar sight, walking miles over cliffs where the gulls wheeled at sunset; visiting villages where old ladies in black clucked like maternal hens at the sight of him, and fed him titbits; chasing basking cats. I felt the soft pressure of his head on my foot, as I read quietly in the evening. An old fisherman on the quay observed, stroking Goofy's ears, "Einai filos me ollous: *He is friend with everybody.*" He could be a handful: in the morning, when lying down on the terrace to start my exercises, I would complain when he clambered all over me. But he learnt quickly; within a week, I found him taking a position exactly parallel to mine. As I stretched forward, one white furry leg stretched out in imitation. I was becoming awfully fond of Goofy.

CHAPTER 2

Not your dog

The heat exploded in August, and Goofy and I started making forays around the island, visiting quiet bays. Many of these were reached down footpaths; others – a worrying sign of tourist incursions – had had rough tracks of broken rocks and shale bulldozed down them. One afternoon, following a new "road" which looked like a prehistoric building site, on a very steep hill, the car had got stuck on the return journey back uphill, wheels turning crazily, scattering debris but not moving an inch forward. After several minutes of this, as the car got infinitely hotter, Goofy jumped straight out through the open window, and in a supreme vote of no confidence in women drivers, made his way up the hill without me. I felt stung by his desertion: finally he had run away. I found something to put under the tyres, and painstakingly nursed the car back up the track. At the very top of the hill, reclining in the cool shade of a eucalyptus tree, sat the dog. I opened the side door, and with a regal air he climbed back in. Obviously, the privilege of looking after Goofy was something that had to be earned.

On the way home I went shopping in the village of Lakka. A car swerved past Goofy, just missing him, and departed in a squeal of tyres and throaty curses. I didn't have Goofy on a lead, because I didn't have one; and because he wasn't my dog. On the island, it was very rare to see a dog walked around on a lead; dogs might be chained up, but at that time the islanders usually let their dogs run free, and took the consequences.

It had been a near miss. I was newly, and painfully, aware of how vulnerable he was. As he clambered into the car with me, banished to the back seat for safety, I thought about what his life – his death – would be like when I'd gone. Goofy sat upright, panting happily on the back seat, and reached up – in one of those joyous bursts of affection that were his trademark – and licked the sea salt on the back of my neck. I felt a wave of worry and responsibility wash over me. Goofy's extraordinary affection made me feel more alive, somehow; but I found that I was no longer carefree.

The next afternoon, I went to a bay to swim; Goofy bounced on the shore, jumping back at the waves, which he seemed not to trust at all. When he suddenly lost sight of me he showed signs of panic. He wavered for a moment; then threw himself into the water, dog-paddling out to me until he had front paws on each of my shoulders, and could lick me ecstatically on the face as I tried to keep us both afloat. Satisfied at last that I wasn't drowning, he paddled his way back to shore. As we settled back into the car, the salt drying on burnt skin and matted fur respectively, I looked at my companion. He was so *game* – and I suddenly felt a pain. If you have ever skimmed pebbles across the surface of the sea, then found a rock and heaved it into the water, it makes a strange bass echoing sound that surprises you. That is what I felt: something had gone deeper than I had expected.

One morning, when I drove to where Goofy's owner worked, Goofy saw where we were heading . . . and hit the floor. He had jumped off the back seat and pressed himself as flat as possible onto the floor of the car, to hide. Two desperate eyes looked up at me, willing me not to betray him.

Perhaps it was inevitable. Gossip is the meat, crusty bread and strong wine of a small Greek village. Spiro used to call the elderly women who sat with his mother by the sea wall on a bench as it grew dark, talking without cease, the "ephemerides" – the newspapers. My canine shadow made me the subject of affectionate village jokes – which must have reached the ears of Goofy's owners. Perhaps they resented all the talk about their dog's marked preference for a foreigner.

17

One peaceful afternoon at the house, Goofy began growling: an unheard-of occurrence. He seemed to recognise the noise of a motorbike, slowly making its way up the track to the house. He scooted under my chair and hid beneath my legs. His owner came up the steps. He had come to take the dog back. Mute, stiff-legged with resistance, Goofy looked at me in desperate entreaty. I had to let him go. He was pulled away by the scruff of the neck. I'd heard rumours of beatings; but there was nothing, absolutely nothing, I could do.

Details of Goofy's life began to emerge. Life for Paxiots falls into two, distinct, summer and winter halves. In winter, it is as cold and wet as England – and you have plenty of time for family and other animals. In summer, you're trying to live a double life – working in the tavernas, the cafes, villa or car hire businesses, until the early hours of the morning, before rising at dawn to do the whole thing all over again. The couple who owned Goofy worked all day, and part of the night, and probably, since they were young, partied thereafter; the dog was left chained, without stimulus. His coat was matted, but there was no mange. He was fed; but he wasn't allowed even the freedom of the garden where he was chained. When I queried this with his young owner, he said it might cause damage to the garden.

Malcolm and Mary had a position in Paxiot life that was as private as it was prestigious. Unlike most of the other English ex-pats, they lived on the island all year round. One saw them much more in winter; in summer, it was understood that they liked to keep themselves to themselves, as the tiny lanes and the little villages became swollen with noise and summer visitors. The locals understood their reticence and treated them with affection. At first sight Malcolm looked like an ancient mariner, sitting on the stone bench reserved for locals at the café, and smoking: a grizzled beard, and thin body in dilapidated vest and dusty shorts. Mary was built more generously, with a long grey plait that swung the whole way down her back, an infectious laugh and strong cheek bones. They surprised the whole village after many years when they invited everyone to a wedding many people had presumed to have taken place decades before. Spiro was their *koumbaros*, or best man: a bond as strong, or stronger, than a blood-tie.

Malcolm levelled his deep eyes at me in response to my greeting. "Have you thought about what you're doing with that dog? I know he's not been looked after properly but you're only going to break his heart when you go away. I've seen it all before. You will only have increased the alienation his owners feel for him, into the bargain. Since you can't see it through, better let the dog alone". I took his warning, painful as it was. I felt chastened. I would return Goofy. But how kind would his owners be to a dog who had made his wish to escape from them so plain? Perhaps, shamefully, I had only made matters worse. I had been a silly woman from abroad, feeding a local cat or dog, until it became attached to me – and had to bear the disappointment of separation and an even harder life. I made a painful resolution; I would avoid Goofy, if I saw him. I would not visit. Maybe his owners and he would settle down together.

Thus began a distressing game of hide and seek all over the island; I was told again and again that Goofy had been seen, looking for me . . . I told myself that he would probably have a much better time at home if he forgot me, but being cruel to be kind was terribly hard. Taking him back when he escaped to me was heartbreaking: the chain he was kept on was so short. The concrete was bare and he was left for hours and hours without stimulus. His owner said that he was unpopular with the neighbours: "He is always screaming," he grimaced. Even if one made allowances for the wrong word in English, this didn't help at all.

A week later, my heart torn by reports from Spiro that the dog had escaped yet again, and had rushed round the village looking for me, I returned late one night to my car, parked in the village by the sea. Something small was curled up in the dark in the dust, below the driver's door. It was Goofy. He had recognised my car, and settled down for the night, in the hope of my return.

CHAPTER 3

Guns and wild carrots

On my return to London, I plunged into city life, but for once it didn't swallow me up. I couldn't settle. Time and time again, I rang Spiro. Had he seen Goofy? Spiro bore patiently with me, shouting dog welfare bulletins over the hubbub of his bar on the jetty, as the season came to a close. When October arrived, so did some real news: Goofy's owners had said they wanted a bigger dog. Spiro thought they might not want Goofy any more. Finally, he said something that made me sick with a new, unfamiliar fear: Spiro thought Goofy's owners might be going to dump him on the mainland. This was a death sentence. There, he might have a lifespan of perhaps a week. If he wasn't run over, Goofy would be shot or poisoned as a stray.

I paced up and down, noting the pale carpets and soft

furnishings around me; all totally unsuitable for a dog who to the best of my knowledge had never been inside a house. Surely it would be impossible to accommodate Goofy in my London flat – let alone my London life. It would be insanity. I took a deep breath, and ran to the phone . . . Spiro scoffed indignantly when I told him to offer Monopoly numbers of drachmas for me, to purchase their unwanted dog from his owners. He protested: *But they throw him away!* After all, if they didn't want the dog . . . but I did not want anything to go wrong. It had to be enough money to make the transaction irrevocable.

Over an hour later, Spiro rang back: Goofy was mine; but he had the unwelcome news that the dog's owners had said they would keep him, until I came to collect him. I said I would completely rearrange my schedule at work, and try to come out immediately; after all, the dog's owners would have no interest in his welfare, after he had negotiated such a spectacular international escape. Perhaps, also, I realised what was expected of me. For some time, I'd had the odd feeling that I was the one who'd been adopted.

As soon as I could, I flew from London to relieve Goofy's owners of their dog. It was out of season and there were no direct flights. What became a typical, and rather expensive, scenario was arrival at 2am at Gatwick; hours of delay before a flight to Athens; hours more to wait before a flight to Corfu; a scramble by taxi to the port, for a ferry or sea taxi to the island. Then I would only have the trek, blinking in the unaccustomed white Greek sunlight, from the main port to the village, with the help of Christos the Taxi.

Shivery with tiredness and trepidation, I hugged Spiro. Exhausted as I was, I still experienced the shock to one's senses that comes with arrival in Greece. The extraordinary Greek light made everything seem brighter, harder to the touch, more immediate. The sky was more vivid; even the dark cyprus trees were shocking in their intensity. In recollection, London in October seemed to have been wrapped in a dingy grey film.

Next morning, Spiro promised, he'd come with me to collect Goofy. I fretted. It had been several months; perhaps the dog would have forgotten me, and I would be taking him against his will? How ludicrous, to rescue a dog who didn't want to go.

Next morning we mounted the hill and went in at the gate. Behind the house, on the short chain I remembered all too well, sat Goofy. As I approached he stared a moment. Then he went beserk. I was nearly torn apart by a frantic, jumping, licking, ecstatic creature. He was making desperate, loving cries as he leapt for me. I was offered the chain, which I declined. Goofy bounded down the hill with us without a backward glance.

We had eight packed days, based at a little apartment in the village. I thought: this dog is brilliant. In the morning sun he'd sit outside on the doorstep, not straying but guarding. At night, he'd curl up with contented sigh at the end of the bed, as I began to tackle the little presents he'd brought me . . . of ticks and fleas. In the first of many challenges to my bank balance, I chartered the sea taxi to take us to Dino the vet in Corfu. Goofy winced against me as the microchip was shot into his shoulder, but stood bravely while the anti-rabies injection followed it. Back in Paxos, Spiro and I discussed Goofy's future at the café in the hills.

It was a café from another time, entire and perfectly preserved. Set among the cyprus trees and eucalyptus, it was a long low building beside the road, with dark green-shuttered windows set like eyes between the open door, fringed by rickety tables and chairs. The Kafeneion sign, hand-painted, was as Greek as the sunshine that had faded it. From inside came the low hum of men's voices and the click of worry beads; this was also the home of good local music. On the walls was a splendid collection of 1930s posters – once again covetable – advertising Papastratos cigarettes; and faded black and white framed photographs of war heroes, braving eternity through bushy moustaches. No EU zone this: a hand-painted wooden board proclaimed that ouzo was still 2 drachmas a glass. Everything was ramshackle; everything was well-loved. Pale green paint adorned the wooden panelling, above an old bare wood floor. On shelves, there was a child's treasury – a funny-shaped pebble here, an ancient calendar there; massive dusty glass jars of sweets. Outside, cats slept in the late autumn sun, ignoring the bluster of passing scooters. Like the massive verdigris church bell hanging from the eucalyptus tree beside the church which faced it, the café seemed to have defied time. Costas, intellectual and gentle, ran it; or perhaps, intransigently Greek as it was, it ran Costas.

Over coffee Spiro said he would look after Goofy for the winter, until the dog was free to enter the UK under our new pet passport scheme. My week was up: next morning Spiro and some other local friends came to say goodbye and he stood on the jetty holding Goofy. As I stepped into the sea taxi, Goofy suddenly saw that I was leaving. He began to strain frantically against the leash. With a desperate effort, he broke free – and I watched in dismay as he hurled himself off the jetty towards my boat. It was too far; he fell into the water. The last thing I saw as the boat pulled away was my dog, swimming desperately and hopelessly in the water towards me, until he was pulled out by a fisherman, sorry and bedraggled.

My cheeks were wet with tears all the way to Athens; memories of that scene were to haunt me as winter took hold of London. I missed my dog badly during those months. I kept finding myself back in Paxos . . . Christmas and New Year; Easter; I yo-yoed back and forth. In December, Goofy and I rented a house above the Eremitis cliffs, stacking huge olive logs on the fire for warmth as the gales made the sea crash on the rocks below. We walked alone in eerie red winter sunsets, two solitary amber figures on the cliffs; but we were not lonely. Greek hospitality reaches its peak at this time, as tavernas and restaurants are closed, and people take it in turns to prepare huge meals for whoever turns up, sending the message 'I'm cooking' by bush telegraph, so that the whole island resembles an itinerant house party.

Millennium night was spent in my favourite tiny ramshackle café, drinking local wine or tequila and orange – both death-defying – as everyone roared out sad songs to the sound of Antonis' mandolin. Time and again the door burst open and another figure appeared, dripping from the storm, with those unfortunate attempts at cake the Greeks adore. Surely it must be midnight by now? Someone noticed that the ancient clock had stopped at quarter to twelve. Every local had had a new plastic digital watch for Christmas, and arguments about the end of the old century threatened the new, until Madame called 'enough!' and physically moved the minute hand, as we counted down to our own, invented midnight. Spiro's protest 'this makes a nonsense of Millennium!' was drowned out by universal hugging and cries of 'chronia pola' – *may you have many years!*

Little wonder I was back again a few days before Greek Easter. I had expected to find the island peaceful, without the incessant noise of summer tourists. In its place, however, was a shock: the air was completely filled instead with birdsong. Instead of dusty roads and stone paths, the tracks were squeezed into narrow footprints, by tumbling waves of green. Goofy and I wandered through wild thyme and cyclamen; intense, heady jasmine, lacy yellow Alexanders, orange blossom and dog roses mixed with the pink and mauve-winged petals of wild peas, which entwined with gorse and yellow broom in the hedgerows. The air was humming to bursting with bees.

To serve with lamb spit-roasted in the open air, Spiro and I picked *horta*, salad weeds and greens, from a natural garden sheltered by trees on the cliff-top. Bright, incredibly fine feathery leaves caught my eye: wild carrot. There was peppery wild rocket; a leaf that tasted of curry and spice; spinach; chard; artichokes; dill and powerful thyme; stepping through the undergrowth released a living potpourri. In the distance, too eager to wait, someone set off an explosion of gunpowder, followed by gun shots. The whole Island was stock-piling explosives, and priming their guns, ready for midnight on Saturday. After poignant and beautiful visits to the Virgin and candle-lit processions, the Paxiots suddenly go mad: in a terrifying cavalcade of shots, explosions and fireworks, often deeply unsafe, they welcome the risen Christ: *Christos anesti!*

That Easter, Goofy had been delighted to see me: at my arrival at Spiro's house, he had hurled himself into my arms, and then got straight into my car to leave. "Little bastard, he didn't even look back", said Spiro, a little hurt. But there was a problem: Goofy was running wild; he was getting into danger. While he had been living with Spiro, he had become adept at chasing motor-bikes and cars. He was also an accomplished killer of chickens. He had been treating Spiro's house as an hotel – staying out all night like some randy teenager, picketing Malcolm and Mary's house across the island when their bitch was in season, only returning to grab some breakfast, then out again . . . When he was caught under the wheel of a Vespa and screamed in pain with an injured back leg, it was obvious that action was overdue. To Spiro's affronted indignation – *you are putting him in a cage* – I arranged for Goofy to stay in kennels at the home of the vet, Dino, who lived with his family high in the Corfu hills. Better safe than sorry. I understood what Spiro meant about imprisonment at the vet's, but at least under the early release scheme, Goofy would evade quar-antine entirely. I worried at how my little nomad would cope with captivity; and I couldn't even see for myself what it was like. I would have to trust Nick the sea taxi to take Goofy to Dino's kennels. My plane was leaving.

CHAPTER 4

Never go anywhere in August

The Greeks have a saying: "*one trouble brings a myriad of others along behind it*". For some reason I'd always had a picture of an evil hunchback, carrying goblins on his shoulders; bringing a series of unexpected and cruelly perverse obstacles into one's path. My first problem arose without my even realising it. I had transported Goofy by sea taxi once again to Corfu, this time for his blood to be taken, to verify that the rabies shot had worked and immunised him. The precious sample was to be sent to Italy, as the British Ministry of Agriculture, about to adopt its Emperor's new clothes as DEFRA, would not accept the findings of any, more local, Greek laboratory. Somehow, in transit, this was lost. Dino the vet could not find my number, so I was unaware that Goofy's exit was no longer on track. I lost three precious months before

Dino managed to tell Nick of the sea taxi about the problem; Nick contacted me and the whole process had to be repeated.

Had I quite realised what lay ahead? Goofy had to be microchipped, given a rabies shot – then return after a month for a blood test, to certify that he was now immune. Then there was another six-month wait before he could be admitted to the UK. Days, hours, mattered. To top off the whole exasperating, worrying process, the dog needed a treatment against ticks and fleas to be administered no more than 48, and no less than 24, hours before admission. This effectively blocked anyone wishing to race by road with their dog from, say southern Italy, through France and onto the ferry. It also started the "vet stop" of stressed, disconsolate pet owners, stuck near Calais while they found an unfamiliar vet to treat their dog for ticks and fleas, and prayed that the resulting papers were in order. I was much cheered by Lady Fretwell, the bright, elegant woman who had masterminded the Passport for Pets campaign; she knew that if we didn't travel with our pets, and push for better access routes, we'd lose the chance.

The second problem: I had discovered my neck was crippled after an injury. It meant an operation, which did not help; and a neck brace. There was no remote possibility that I could drive with my neck in a brace all the way through France and Italy to Greece, to pick up Goofy, and bring him home. We would have to risk flights in the middle of August; the worst possible time to transport a dog. I thought I should go alone; partly because it was the sort of nightmare journey I couldn't inflict on a friend; partly because not in my most pessimistic forebodings did I realise what lay ahead.

If the British share anything with the Greeks, it is a love of petty bureaucracy. I was in full combat mode: I bought a small black old-fashioned Greek notebook, the sort with a stout black elastic band to keep its pages together, and crammed its dozens of pages with telephone numbers, locator numbers, document details, prescribed crate sizes for Goofy in an airline hold. I had a folder bulging with certificates, test results ... no wonder my neck felt sore; it was difficult to hold it above the waves of paperwork.

At last it was time for Goofy to come to England. It was an August cursed with the sort of sullen, brutal heatwave that makes shock newspaper headlines. Arriving exhausted and dirty at midnight in Corfu, I checked into a hotel for a couple of hours' rest, too troubled to sleep: I set a 5am alarm. I'd been promised on the phone by Air Cargo in Corfu that they'd be open at 7am, so I could arrange for them to issue Goofy's ticket, the precious waybill, from Corfu to Athens, and a transfer flight from Athens to Heathrow. Given the conditions it was absolutely essential we travel on the same flight; otherwise I'd be unable to check if he were still surviving.

I arrived at six thirty at the concrete hut near the airport that served as an office and waited three hours, like an unwanted and grubby vagrant on the tarmac outside. The heat was already considerable before I discovered they had misinformed me, and wouldn't open till Monday. I faced defeat: my own, non-transferable ticket was for Wednesday morning, and inexplicably they wanted more than 48 hours' notice before flight to issue a waybill.

My hotel wouldn't let a dog paw cross the threshold, so I hired an open jeep to collect Goofy for the day from Dino; I would have to return him in the evening. Given the pain from my neck, so much driving was not ideal. Dino's village was in the Corfiot hills; his pretty house had a high-fenced garden of orange and lemon trees and jasmine, which led onto an expanse of land with kennels and pens. I searched and listened. No Goofy . . . I ran from kennel to kennel until Dino appeared. Goofy, it appeared, was not in an outside kennel. Goofy was *indoors*. My little dog had so charmed his way into the hearts of Dino's wife and son that within a week of arrival, he had been allowed into their home.

During the day I drove miles with the dog strapped in a harness like a merry fighter pilot; then I drove back for an hour, to return him to the vet at night. Dino reported that Goofy had been challenging the resident Alsatians, and was so combative that he couldn't be walked with them; did I know that he was an Alpha dog, and potentially a problem? "But I have been watching you with him", he said. "Somehow, I have a feeling that you will be all right."

On Monday, there was a nice man at Air Cargo, the concrete office near Corfu airport. He bent the rules a little, but to no avail, because he couldn't raise his Athens office at all on the telephone. He said that perhaps they'd all gone swimming . . . I finally got them myself on my mobile, and handed it over to my new friend. He reported that now, apparently, there wasn't space for Goofy on my flight. I was desperate that we travel together, so it was back to the airport, for more queuing, obstruction and hassle. At last it was agreed that Goofy and I would both fly the first step at dawn.

Next Dino discovered that as a private vet, he couldn't issue the last vital element – a Greek export certificate. It needed a 'state listed' vet. The only one available was going away in 45 minutes, and wouldn't wait. There was no map, but he said I'd find it in town near the prison. It was only when gridlocked in traffic in boiling heat, with the minutes rushing away, that I realised I didn't know the Greek for prison. With horns blaring behind me, I rang Paxos on my mobile. "Help! What's the word for prison?". "Jesus Christ, Belinda, what have you done?" Passers-by couldn't help. A total stranger obligingly got in the jeep to direct me, but he didn't know either. Never had a lecherous tribute to my tanned bare legs been so unwelcome.

Finally a dour vet stamped reams of paper. I returned, drained, to check out from the hotel, and headed to the vet's to collect the crate that was to house Goofy en route. It was massive. When it was in place I couldn't see out of the back or sides of the jeep and lugging it on board finished off my damaged neck.

At dawn, once again Olympic Airways at Corfu airport didn't want to know us. I persevered. I insisted we had tickets, waybills and documents. We were both to fly to Athens, where Goofy would be released to me to wait, before checking in six hours later for London.

Is there anything worse than that sinking feeling as you're waiting at the luggage carousel, and everyone else seems to have got their bag? When your luggage is alive, you begin to feel panic. I started a long, frustrating trawl through Athens airport. No-one wanted to help. My worst nightmare was unfolding; Goofy was lost somewhere in Athens, alone and trapped in heat. It was already 40° C.

The woman at Information couldn't say where Goofy was, but admitted perhaps he was in Cargo. He shouldn't be in Cargo – could I find out? "It is not permitted". Where was Cargo? "Not permitted." I explained I had top authority permission to inspect the dog and brandished the documents I'd bound in a leather folder with an embossed crest. The crest actually said 'Formula One 50th Anniversary', from a charity dinner I had organised, but luckily she wasn't a motor racing fan. She rang someone in charge of Cargo without result, and to my exasperation she would give me the name but not the address of the building. She added unhelpfully that it was 20 minutes' drive away. That left a wide margin for error.

Outside I flagged down a taxi, and showed the driver the name. Did he know it? "No", he said. I got in.

Vangelis the taxi driver was a dog lover. We arrived at a depressing series of warehouses, like the ugly back end of an industrial estate, with the squalor of long neglect that Dickens would have recognised. There was no door or entry point from the road, so I climbed over a plank of wood to get inside a loading dock, praying Vangelis wouldn't leave me stranded. The woman in charge was locked in a glass office; she was as hard and impassive as a prison governor. She didn't speak English, but desperation fuelled my Greek. I proudly introduced her to Formula One, and she reluctantly started making calls. No sign of any dog. She called a man off a fork lift truck, and abandoned me to him. He was Turkish. In total mutual incomprehension we started searching past disintegrating pallets and miles of boxes. I have never seen anywhere more devoid of hope: mile upon mile of piled-up yellow crumbling magazines, decades late; rotting boxes, never delivered.

Eventually, in a corner, I saw a single luggage chariot – and a familiar blue crate.

Goofy's whole crate must have been turned over. His spill-proof water bowl was broken; his bedding was soaked and he had no water. I rectified this, and walked him up and down as long as I dared.

Back at the airport, I was pessimistic. The crate wouldn't be loaded, and Goofy would be abandoned, imprisoned, and die slowly in the heat. As I boarded the plane, I headed straight for the cockpit, to ask the captain to confirm my dog was in the hold – the right part of the hold. No time to be shy and retiring now. For three nerve-wracking hours, as my British fellow passengers loudly treated their sunburns and hangovers with gin and tonics, I sat thinking about what might be happening in that hold. Before we landed, I called the stewardess, and asked that Heathrow be notified to have their animal reception van on standby on the tarmac: there was a dog on the plane.

CHAPTER 5

Mutt in Mayfair

"What a poppet!" said a large friendly kennel maid, as Goofy skedaddled in, so eager to escape that he was skating on the floor. It was four days later, and I had driven to the Berkshire kennels which had received Goofy from Heathrow. They had been kind to me, as well as to Goofy; they had liaised with Dino the vet in Corfu when – in one of the most cruel tricks fate could dream up – it looked as if the dog would have to serve six months in prison anyway: there was a discrepancy in the name of the drug on the rabies certificate and on Dino's vaccination form. Dino kindly saved us from disaster by driving into his surgery at night, to fax an excuse of clerical error, which the authorities accepted.

Goofy was fit as a fiddle. After giving me an ecstatic hello, he charged out of his own little prison block, and pulled me around the quarantine kennels. Whilst in his pen, he would have heard the mournful cries of some of the long-term inmates; it seemed he wanted to visit them. He approved wholeheartedly of my new car, and after a few stern instructions from me to lie down in his new bed, in the rear of the hatchback, all was well. The Goofy wagon had passed the test.

I had prepared for the new arrival. I would introduce Goofy to the country, first: I took a few days off work and drove him from the kennels to the tiny cottage I had rented in Wiltshire, where we could acclimatise to one another before facing London.

In anticipation of Goofy's arrival, I had rented the cottage earlier that year. It was in a part of Wiltshire quite unlike the long, bare plains around Stonehenge. This was a place of green undulations: dense woods of hazel, oak and beech; underfoot, as the seasons changed, one walked through winter aconites, bluebells and wild garlic. It was a wild place of lapwings and barn owls and shy deer. Everywhere there was a sense of freedom, of clean space. It moved me with a passion that I had never expected. I knew we would be happy here.

At the cottage, Goofy raced round the tiny garden, then bounded inside and up the stairs. In the bedroom, carefully and gravely, he cocked one leg – and wet the foot of the bed. I showed my disapproval with a deep theatrical sigh of sorrow; I feared we were in for months of toilet training, and knew I should not start by being confrontational. Goofy looked apologetic, which he could do eloquently. Never again did he soil the house. It seemed to be something symbolic: a definitive marking of his territory, once and for all.

On Goofy's second English country morning, we were woken by torrential rain. I opened the back door to let the dog out. He stopped on the threshold and teetered on the edge, peering. I received a dirty look: *You don't go out in this, do you?* No call of nature was urgent enough. He turned his tail on me and went back to bed.

He soon learnt that the disadvantages of the English weather were compensated for by the countryside: he seemed exultant as we walked along hedgerows, shoulder-high cow parsley waving as we passed. We traced a Neolithic path high across the lip of curved hills to an Iron Age hill fort. Goofy, the dog from Paxos, was literally in his element: he breasted the long grasses in the meadows like a child jumping waves. He seemed to know intuitively how to start pheasants up like sky-rockets, and he pounced on rabbits. I even found him, when I went blackberrying, taking a ripe berry carefully with his teeth to avoid the brambles.

And I – in looks, I was transformed. Very interesting muscles appeared on my legs from hours of dog walking. Gone was the soignée siren who tried so hard in designer suits; I had developed a ruddy, abandoned look, in shapeless mac and muddy boots, trailing not perfume, but dog hairs.

At night, a routine was established for me. Goofy liked to retire by 10.30pm. I would hear him slowly jumping the stairs upstairs, and if I was still downstairs after an hour, there would be bumping steps down again; he had come to ask me what I thought I was doing. As I got into bed to read, he would wait until I turned off the light. Then the sound of couple of steps, followed by an almighty flying leap onto the end of the bed. There was a deep sigh, followed a few minutes later by contented little clickings, licking of lips and, if I could have seen them in the dark, working paws and eyebrows. These dreams were vivid. Sometimes he seemed to be eating; sometimes there were little moans of perplexity; and, in the early weeks, there were terrible nightmares: whines and suppressed cries that seemed to wrack him so badly that I sometimes woke him gently, stroking him until he was calm.

Next stop London, where Goofy assimilated as if he'd known all along he'd fit in. He quickly made Mayfair his patch, a cheerful mutt among the pedigree population. Goofy would sniff appreciatively as we passed Allens the butchers, purveyors by appointment of fine bones. He presided happily over my office, and made dog friends in Hyde Park. Almost immediately, everyone in the neighbourhood seemed to know him. He learnt English ("Goofy, don't even *think* it") as well as Greek. "You're bi-woofal, you are," said the postman, fondling his ears.

We had a little battle of wills over getting into the car. Goofy was perfectly able to jump into the back of my Volkswagen, but wouldn't; he preferred me to lift him, which covered my business clothes in mud. *"Mesa"* – *inside* – I would say firmly, as he understood the command. *"Mesa!"* I repeated several times. It was a stand-off. A worker on the building site opposite called out. "My money's on the dog, love . . ."

Very unusually for a dog, Goofy looked one straight and openly in the eyes; he actually studied people's expressions. The short Queen Anne legs gave him a perky, comical look, and he carried himself very proudly, which made people smile. When begging for food, he was a master. He learnt quickly that the taxi rank near our home housed a nomadic tribe of drivers who would rest on the rank whilst waiting for fares from the hotel, sharing anecdotes and eating bacon sandwiches. Ordinary mortals would hesitate to interrupt this cabal off duty, but Goofy soon won his right to be seated beside the cabbie in the cab itself, helping him to polish off the bacon. There was something very touching about the tenderness with which these big men spoke to my dog.

I had presumed that central London would be particularly unfriendly to a dog with Goofy's background. But I could not have brought him to a better place. At that time, Mayfair was still a village, that swelled and swirled during the day with well-heeled visitors. Tired shoppers trudged from Bond Street with carrier bags; frail old ladies in fur coats walked unsteadily with their tiny treasured lapdogs; Arabs swept past in limousines with darkened windows; stick-thin models, cantilevered over high heels, stepped gawkily into hairdressers. It reverted to its essentials when they departed; at weekends, it was as quiet as if the Bomb had dropped.

Behind the scenes it was a gloriously idiosyncratic place, full of characters. It had secrets: little tucked-away green squares, and, seconds from my home, Mount Street Gardens, one of London's loveliest hidden spaces. Goofy adored the sociability of town; each lamp-post had to receive a daily message. We peeped into art gallery windows and ventured into Shepherds Market, the raffish maze of little walkways, tiny bars and restaurants. One could walk a dog everywhere. In the early morning, Goofy would find his friend the road sweeper sitting on a bench in the gardens, and sit beside him, giving him affectionate kisses in exchange for pieces of cheese roll from a battered tuck box.

The shops in Mount Street were still mainly family businesses, not the packaged chains which have now flattened the character out of British streets. Mount Street had a complete world: butcher; poulterer; pub; chemist; post office; optician; cleaners; tobacconist with cigars; stationers and printers; tailors . . . when Goofy arrived, they were thriving and seemingly inhabited by dog lovers. At the optician's, three little dogs romped with Goofy while I had my eyes tested; first thing in the morning,

Goofy would visit Audie, his particular friend and her boss, the funny, perceptive and laconic tailor Doug Hayward. He frolicked through the shop, as a parade of Doug's celebrity regulars sat on the kilim-covered sofa, for a chat: Terence Stamp, Michael Parkinson, Alan Whicker, the photographer Terry O'Neill . . . It was a meeting place where they gleaned information; much, I think, as Goofy sniffed lamp posts. One morning Goofy and I went in for a bit of company, and came out with the name of a first-rate removals man, a first night review of a new show, and the truth behind a prime piece of society gossip.

Last thing night at Goofy made a farewell tour of his patch: he would go to the back door of the kitchens of the Richoux café, and if I wasn't quick, the tender-hearted manageress would have a big sausage waiting for him. At Harry's Bar, where the owner had made Goofy a member, Mark the doorman would sneak out cheese straws, or a slice of mortadella, in between ushering guests into the inner sanctum. Finally, in Serafino, the family ristorante in Mount Street, Goofy would demand two amaretti biscuits, unwrapped from their paper, for dessert. As he grew older, I gradually got his fans to substitute less fattening treats; but neither they, nor Goofy, could bear for him to be deprived altogether.

Day by day, as Goofy took over my life, I became more and more aware of my responsibility for looking after him; he became still more tenderly precious to me. One intensely bright December morning, when Hyde Park was iced and sparkling, I looked at a pair of geese flying away overhead and found my cheeks were wet with tears – from imagining losing Goofy. This wouldn't do, I told myself. You should be fantasising about what you'll do when you are free . . .

There had only been one real scare. A few days after he'd arrived I went to a doctor's appointment, leaving Goofy in the office. A motorbike messenger let him out while nobody noticed, and he set off to find me. Visions of a small dog with no traffic sense crossing Park Lane made my heart stop. If he survived, he could be lost to me forever; his identity disc was still being engraved. A whole hour of searching revealed that he'd been taken away by two women in Grosvenor Square.

It was Daniel, the young doorman at the Connaught Hotel, who saved the day. Two women passed, one carrying a dog. "Madam", he said, as if surprised she didn't know, "*that is Goofy*".

CHAPTER 6

We want the dog story

Shortly after I brought Goofy to London, I gave a lift in my car to a friend who worked in newspapers. My mind was full of the extraordinary thing that had happened to me since we'd last met, and I told her all about Goofy. How marvellous he was; how agonizing it had been to bring him back; how he had changed me permanently from the metropolitan girl she had known when we were both students at Oxford. I was not at all prepared when she rang me next morning from her office, after an editorial conference. "Belinda," she said "We want the dog story!"

I was reluctant. I had written some journalism, but nothing as personal and revealing as this. I remembered how Dorothy Parker had once reviewed Winnie the Pooh: "*I fwowed up*"; there was a sneering, cynical world out there and I was exposing myself to a reputation for soppiness. On the other hand, there was still much to do to persuade Government to adopt sensible measures on pet travel. So I wrote about the little dog who had changed me, and all the pitfalls of rescuing an animal from overseas.

When his story appeared one Saturday morning, my odd little dog had become a celebrity. People in the park came up to me – *is that Goofy?* A week later the editor himself sought me out. "I have a *Bonio* to pick with you, Belinda", he said dryly. He had delivered himself in that same Saturday edition of a controversial pronouncement on foreign policy and predicted confidently to his colleagues that there would be a massive post bag in response. He had been highly gratified by the avalanche of letters that arrived – until they all turned out to have been written by people congratulating him on running the story of "that plucky, adorable dog . . ." It was so good, said his readers, to have some good news in the paper for once; a sentiment to which most journalists are allergic. To add to his chagrin, several enclosed a dog biscuit.

In my office, I suddenly found that I was Goofy's agent. A producer called from Gloria Hunniford's TV chat show, Open House – would Goofy appear as their guest? TV studios are a come-down to those who have never seen them before. This one resembled a warehouse with concrete floors, more than a "house"; the set was cunningly and cheaply constructed of painted flats and screens.

Gloria Hunniford's Open House had a jolly, mainly middle-aged, female audience. Goofy exceeded all expectations: from the moment he arrived in the Green Room for some hospitality, he was on his very best behaviour; he was neither over-excited nor uncooperative.

Gloria Hunniford was charming. Had she known that Goofy had identified "rat runs" round the walls (as most studios have a permanent audience of rats and mice) she might have been less sanguine. I feared that our cosy armchair chat on camera might be punctuated by Goofy leaping into the audience, and returning with something struggling and bloody in his jaws. I needn't have worried; ever the showman, as soon as Goofy felt the warmth coming from the audience –a ripple of soft sound, from the more tender-hearted of the women – he behaved like an angel.

Goofy was a hit – something that understandably did not thrill the redoubtable actress Patricia Routledge, who had been asked to join Gloria Hunniford to discuss her new West End role as Lady Bracknell in *The Importance of Being Earnest*. Used as I was since childhood to watching celebrity shows like Parkinson and Wogan, I knew that the biggest star got the final interview; the others were merely warm-ups to the big name. What Patricia Routledge felt on discovering that she was playing second billing to a dog, was never divulged; but her eyes, when she was introduced to us, were not warm.

Goofy was recognized immediately when we took our

walks in Hyde Park. There was something very simple about Goofy and his story – hurling himself off the jetty to try to swim for my boat as I left – that touched people. The dog had suddenly become a celebrity; he still came to the office every day, a stress-reliever and a comfort – and now, sometimes, he was the reason that the office phones were ringing.

I received a call from the producer of Richard and Judy – then an ITV morning programme with an audience of millions. The seemingly indelible duo had an enormously powerful show which ran from early morning until lunchtime. It was true that it would help our little pet travel advisory service, but this, I felt, was getting ridiculous. We had got away with Gloria, but the prospect of Goofy on the Richard and Judy sofa aroused in me a wicked fear. Would he be the first of their celebrity guests to lick his own genitals live on TV?

The night before our big interview, I put out my best trouser suit, having thought that my skirts might ride up if I had to make a sudden lunge to prevent Goofy from humping Richard Madeley. I then had friends round for drinks – lots of friends, and lots of drinks. In the early hours, my alarm sounded. Dawn brought pouring rain and a sickly hangover, compounded by an attack of nerves. There was a chauffeured car waiting outside to transport us to the studios. We swayed through dark, unfriendly streets. As if in a disjointed trance, I was shown along a corridor in the studios to a dressing room.

He was – debatably – a spaniel.

Summers were spent in the country.

When he was naughty, he was eloquent.

. . . to one who had greatness of heart.

It had the name GOOFY on the door in massive letters, with "and Belinda Harley" in much smaller letters beneath it: an A-list celebrity and his D-list minder. The small room was bare except mirror, coffee cups and water; nothing to keep a dog from fretting. We sat quietly and longed for bed, until a researcher came in and announced that we would be 'on' nearer *midday*. When I protested about the effect of hours and hours of incarceration on the dog, she said we might be needed earlier, for trailers. After we had investigated different bare corridors, I decided that we would escape for a walk.

We tried to battle our way along the walkway by the Thames, past the National Theatre, Festival Hall and Westminster Bridge, buffeted by gales. My mac was blown around me like a tattered, useless sail, the precious trouser suit now clung to me like a drenched and clammy rag; and Goofy's little white furry skirts at the business end of him were blown backwards as we walked with the wind behind us. The darkest sky that I had ever seen opened, and a monsoon of freezing rain drowned us. My boots squelched like pulp, my hair hung down in rats' tails; Goofy, too, looked like a disaster victim – fur slicked onto his body by the downpour till he looked smaller and somehow naked. Then my mobile phone rang in my pocket: it was the studio. We were needed urgently.

I ran with Goofy through dirty puddles. The studio staff took one look at Goofy and rushed him to Make-up; I watched as the dog was given an emergency blow-dry to restore his coat to snowy, fluffy perfection, while I was left damp as we were led onto the studio floor. "Sit on that low step, love, and ask the dog to stand up on his back legs and put one paw on each of your shoulders and look at you, please", said the director, who seemed to have spent thirty years without meeting any dogs. Goofy, however, had turned rather protective of me and, astonishingly, complied to the letter, which the studio staff mistook for trained obedience. In the course of the next couple of hours, we were summoned several times to strike coy, unnatural poses, and I began to feel rather stroppy. At last, we were ushered onto the set, and it turned out that Richard Madeley was to be our interviewer.

Many years previously, I had taken the great Peter Ustinov to the north, to launch a morning TV programme – and they had practised the same trick of insisting the great man get all the way to Liverpool at dawn, and then forced him to sit through hours of trivial interviews with other people. Ustinov and I sat forlorn and ignored in a corner, eating fudge ("have some more, Belinda; luckily I don't *have* a metabolism"). Instead of Peter Ustinov, they preferred to interview to a young man with slicked-back hair who proceeded to show an entire new range of Brylcreem products. It seemed to me like product endorsement; why keep Ustinov waiting for this? We got to our feet for Peter's turn, but no – they introduced a worthy woman who bought Marks and

Spencer cardigans, and then embroidered flowers on them. At last, as I was threatening that we would have to leave, they introduced a very tired Peter Ustinov – and proceeded to usher him in with the theme tune to The Pink Panther: one of the few movies of the period in which he had played no part at all. "Well, Sir Peter", said the interviewer with a satisfied smile. "You've been in the studio watching the programme this morning; have you any questions you would like to ask?" "Yes," said Peter. "How do I get Brylcreem stains off cardigans?"

It's awful, how cruel they are to animals over there, isn't it?" began Madeley, chummily. "Actually", I said, churlishly, "I think that whilst there's a lot of cruelty in Greece, at least it is out in the open; here, in England, it goes on too, but behind closed doors". This wasn't the answer he had hoped for, perhaps, and I began to feel I wasn't playing the game. I felt ashamed; damp, cold, and foolish too. I had noticed that the trailers had suggested I was some Shirley Valentine, out in Greece to find a man, who had come home with a dog instead. Somehow at the end they seemed delighted with the interview; when I queried this, they reassured me it had all been wonderful. Goofy, they said, had been terrific.

CHAPTER 7

Learning my lessons

"D'you know, I think I'm losing it", said Jamie, who ran the flower stall at the corner of the Grosvenor Chapel, beside my office. "I'm definitely losing it". Jamie had offered to look after Goofy while I visited the dentist. He had left him briefly tethered at the stall, while he walked across the road to the takeaway sandwich booth. He looked down at Goofy. "When I got back, I found not only had I bought two Bakewell tarts – I'd bought *two teas* . . ."

Jamie raised an eyebrow when I told him that Goofy and I had been to dog training class, and that in front of all the other dogs, Goofy had obeyed the *sit, stay* and *lie down* first time. I offered a demonstration; but Goofy looked at me with disdain: no big audience, no need . . . I came to understand that my dog did what he was told, but only to oblige me, and purely out of love. It was an affectionate concession. It was not what dog training manuals required – but all in all, it served us.

It was also the professional consensus that a dog who once had to live by begging, could not just ditch the habit when requested. It was his proven survival tactic; and therefore, probably, ineradicable. I took this excuse for my failure to improve him with relief. Peter the vet at Keith Butt's surgery sighed, as he obediently fed Goofy twice the usual ration of treats allowed per patient, when Goofy demanded them. "Gosh", he said, "If this were my dog, he'd be circular".

On one of my lunchtime walks with Goofy, he spotted in the far distance the russet corduroy knickerbockers of Hill House school children, this time a class of little girls playing rounders. He streaked over to the game, leaving me standing many yards behind. A little fair girl, no more than twelve years old, attracted him. I saw him playfully putting his paws on her front, and then I broke into a run. It was his rogering position – Goofy was rubbing himself up against her. As I joined the group, there were pubescent, smutty giggles and squeals from the other girls. Then a shrill whistle pierced the air and the games mistress, in cut-glass tones, called out in a doomed stage whisper "*Jessicah, stand perfectly still*". She sounded as horrified as if Goofy had pulled a gun; in terms of propriety, he had. As the class continued to snigger, I apologetically pulled him off, and I slunk away with my unrepentant little sex pervert.

Dogs, like men, make enemies among their own kind. With certain dogs Goofy made friends; with others, he turned instantly into a prize fighter – taunting and ready for a scrap. His particular bête noir was black and tan – a small, uncontrollable Jack Russell called Jack, who went into a frenzy of barking as Goofy approached. As a puppy, Jack had a habit of placing his claws close to Goofy's eyes – and after warning growls were ignored, I am afraid Goofy bit his ear. The two had shouting matches as soon as they saw one another, yards away. As the older, wilier adversary, Goofy would deliver a single bark up against the letter box as we passed Jack's house. Within seconds this was followed by a tremendous thud, as the body of an enraged Jack Russell slammed against the inside of the front door, and the house erupted in a fury of barking, the noise of which followed us down several streets as Goofy sauntered along, quietly delighted with his handiwork.

Once we met Jack in Hyde Park, when to my anxiety and that of his owner – a dear friend – both dogs were off the lead. Goofy came to my call, and passed up the opportunity for a real fight. I was immensely pleased and proud of him. As a reward, I headed into a different part of the park, and we spent an extra three-quarters of hour playing together in deep mutual contentment. Our walk home took us past Jack's house: Goofy started up to the front door as usual – and then I saw him stop and consider. He'd seen Jack out in the park – and Jack had been heading away from home. No point in barking if Jack wasn't in . . . To my astonishment, for the one and only time, Goofy refrained from barking out a challenge. It seemed he had retained the memory of Jack in the park; associated it with the house; and acted upon the conclusion. I was impressed.

Ted was the concierge at a block of flats a few yards from my office. He was the mildest of men: I had met him "exercising" a fat, disgruntled-looking King Charles spaniel in Hyde Park. If Ted threw a ball for it, it sauntered over in the right direction, but mostly they just sat on a bench together and went nowhere. In the camaraderie of dog owners – who are introduced as friends by their dogs, when we would otherwise be shy of conversation with strangers – Ted told me the King Charles belonged to people in the flats he managed, and he very conscientiously got it to move a little, during his lunch hour. He said how he envied me Goofy, so keen to explore and stretch his legs. I agreed, ruefully; Goofy's lunch-time walks played havoc with my social life. The restaurants I no longer visited! The business information I no longer exchanged; the world of delicious exploration which beckoned in the simple words "let's have lunch". Nowadays, lunch was a swift dash into the glass self-service cafeteria by the Serpentine, returning to the dog outside with a pallid sandwich which we shared in the rain.

Gradually, Ted took over some of my lunchtime walks

with Goofy. I'm afraid Goofy repaid Ted's devotion by treating him like a servant. When Goofy wanted to go out, Ted was summoned by an impatient bark. If for some reason Goofy didn't want to leave me, he would run back upstairs to my office, deserting Ted at the back door. Ted would give him treats of encouragement to go downstairs again. I was aware that one shouldn't give in to blackmail, and ordered Goofy out sternly. Ted explained that once they reached the park, I was forgotten, but Goofy's pleading reluctance made me anxious all through lunchtime until I heard him bounding up the stairs on his return.

After a walk with Ted, dog discipline evaporated. For a while I was puzzled by this, but then I discovered that when out with Ted, Goofy insisted on his own preferred route. He would not go where Ted wanted; he pulled Ted round, and at several key points on the walk, he would sit immobile, bottom firmly down, *and refuse to move until given a biscuit.* He had exploited Ted's gentleness to place him lower in the pack. What I got back each afternoon was a canine dictator.

Things were different when Ted came to my flat to dog-sit. It was lads' night: I would leave Ted and Goofy sitting side by side on the sofa, watching the big football match on TV – with beer, crisps and dog snacks within reach.

When I dressed up in the evenings, Goofy would react with a deep sigh of disapproval if he saw a pair of high heels. High heels meant dinner parties, which were usually dog free zones; he approved of boots, suitable for dog-walking. Early on in my life as a canine spinster, I went to the white tie annual Royal Academy Dinner, and Goofy not only gave me a wintry look as I climbed into a long dress; he struggled towards me, eyes pleading and groaning. Decidedly off colour. Worse still, his favourite supper lay untouched. In consternation I left Ted a note asking him to keep a close eye on the dog, and ring me on my mobile so that I could rush back at any moment.

The dinner was long, the speeches longer – but then I had the chance of drinks in a party which contained Sir David Attenborough . . . Very sadly I gave my apologies: *I'm afraid I have a sick dog at home.* I hurled myself out of the taxi, heart racing. Waiting for me was a revelation. "Belinda, I don't know what you were talking about! Goofy wolfed his supper as soon as I arrived, and has dragged me round the entire neighbourhood". It had been a try-on . . .

Thereafter, the balance of power had to be adjusted regularly; as he got older, he wanted me more and more. When I had the temerity to go away for a week, he wouldn't eat for three days in kennels, and only cheered up when they introduced a bitch to his quarters. He sent me to Coventry for two whole days on my return. At the cottage, if I had to go out in the evening, Goofy would settle near the back door to wait for me. If I was longer than an hour, he would go into the sitting-room. There he was allowed on the sofa; but a small pale yellow arm-chair was off limits, and he knew it. As I opened the door quietly on my return, I would hear the unmistakable sound of a dog jumping off a forbidden armchair.

CHAPTER 8

By Appointment

Vice-Admiral Sir James Weatherall had commanded the Ark Royal, and now sat in St James's Palace as Her Majesty's Marshal of the Diplomatic Corps, where he was responsible for all the Ambassadors at the Court of St. James's. He was as big, bluff and friendly as a character from Hornblower. His grand office was below my own tiny pigeonhole in St. James's Palace, when I worked there. He and his wife Jean were immensely sociable and kind. *Brazil, come and meet Denmark!* Jean would cry, having long since dispensed with Ambassadors' real names in the welter of diplomatic changeovers. Like a kindly housemaster helping the new boys, Jim's eyes would twinkle as he explained the arcane snobberies and rituals of life in London over impressive measures of alcohol. They also gave dinner parties, and as a single girl, I was invited to make up numbers if a new Ambassador were widowed or single. I was slightly thrown to discover that my first blind date was the Papal Nuncio.

At dinner, Jim asked me to talk about bringing my dog into Britain. This was something that caused anguish to diplomatic families: being posted to London meant a beloved family pet being shut up for six months in quarantine, from which some never recovered; one Ambassador, since his dog was too old to cope, had had the animal put down. Jim offered to host a reception in St James's for ambassadors to meet Lady Fretwell and the Passports for Pets people. Goofy was invited, too.

It was the big evening, and I mingled nervously at the Ambassadors' reception. When Jim asked me to mount the small platform and say a few words about pet travel, Goofy – who had been introducing himself to the Highland terrier owned by Jim's secretary – must have heard my voice. He made his way though the crowd, and jumped onto on the platform beside me. He sat at my feet, then deliberately placed one paw on my shoe, looking up at his mistress's voice to a chorus of delighted, sentimental *aaahs* from the diplomats.

My little office in London was now providing a rudimentary pet travel advisory service. We had discovered a pet chauffeur: a man of Herculean unflappability with an air conditioned vehicle; he would drive your pets from Biarritz to Bognor if necessary, with stops en route for walks and food, with border documents, tick and flea treatment included.

Malaga to Manchester was a very popular route. Many British people retire to Spain; when one partner dies and the survivor cannot cope alone and must return to England, there is often an equally elderly cat or dog, the last member of the "family", who would not survive a flight, let alone quarantine. Here our pet chauffeur was a godsend; he sometimes drove the pensioner, too. One summer, he drove a woman writer home from France, in a gloriously eccentric convoy with her car, containing a mêlée of dogs, books and local red wine.

Perhaps most touching of all, I heard about a merchant ship which made a month-long passage from Shoreham on the South coast, to the Falklands; on board, individual seamen would each take personal charge of a dog "passenger" – a pet from a family posted overseas. There must have been bonds forged between man and dog on that little ship, where pooches ran up and down the decks; and a manly pang or two when the dog was taken away by grateful owners on the other side of the world.

It was lucky that Travelpets, our little service, gave us such delightful insights into human nature: it yielded nothing in the way of profit. It was possibly the worst business idea I had ever dreamt up. For a small annual membership fee supposed to cover costs, pet owners could run up many hundreds of pounds' worth of time and administration in setting up a complicated journey overseas – and then, at the last minute, cancel their travel plans entirely. Many months were spent researching how to get Lauren Bacall's tiny dog Sophie from the US to the Connaught Hotel. Miss Bacall wanted her beside her on the plane. The London route on Concorde would not help, nor other carriers to the UK. Frequently, this was not a matter of passenger safety, or anything other than the airline being reluctant to take extra trouble; the French often did it with cheerful ease. Finally, we suggested to Miss Bacall's assistant that she could fly First Class to Paris, with Sophie in the cabin with her – and we would arrange to have them met at the barrier in France. While Miss Bacall took a plane on to London, our dog chauffeur would transport the precious cargo to the Connaught, door to door. After many weeks it was still not good enough, and eventually we heard no more.

Months later, Goofy and I were passing the entrance to the Connaught when suddenly Goofy leapt into the porch with a fearsome bark, ready to scrap. It was a miniscule canine: the sort that sports little bows in its hair. Goofy wasn't attacking; it was purely bluster – but there was an ear-splitting screech of "*Sophie . . .*" and an angular form, familiar in the disconcerting way that older film stars often are, swooped down. There were the cheekbones, now jutting in anger, that had captivated Bogart. I scolded Goofy and pulled him away. He looked up at me, an unrepentant rogue. *Sophie, heh?*

CHAPTER 9

In which we are rescued

The only time that Mark Birley, that quintessentially reserved Englishman, sent me a love letter, it began . . . "Darling Belinda, I know I only saw you last night, and will see you again in a few days, but there is something I wanted to put in writing. I want to tell you how much I love and admire you" (here, I caught my breath) "*for rescuing that divine dog*". The rest of the letter was not about me at all. It was all about Goofy.

At the time I met him, Mark Birley was the creator and irresistible force behind three private clubs which dominated London high life. An international set clung to him: people longed to be recognized, to belong. Mark was six foot four, with an extraordinary masculine beauty. His voice was deep, and rippled with sardonic humour. We had two vital things in common: a sense of humour and a very good appetite. Mark maintained his clubs to a level of perfection that is no longer seen: it demanded ceaseless work and attention to detail. I often thought that by indulging his own tastes, he gave a great deal more to the world than many more public-spirited individuals. In private, he was the sort of man who has been driving women demented for generations; but he was a magnificent friend. He was also a dog man: many said of Mark that he was only really at ease with his dogs. When most of my friends sighed over my folly in rescuing Goofy, Mark alone got the point. If we shared a mutual infatuation, it was, in its finest points, canine.

One night in the country, alone with Goofy, I had had an accident. With Goofy pulling me energetically on the lead, I had tripped on some stone steps. One hand was full of dog lead, the other held bag and keys, so I smashed onto a bare stone floor without hands free to break my fall. In the early hours a dear friend responded to my SOS, and drove me gingerly to London, to hospital. It was obvious that I had done something serious – and there was only time to stop at Mark's house en route, and entrust Goofy to Elvira, his housekeeper. Mark at that time had three dogs – Bella, the Alsatian; Jennifer, an elderly black Labrador, and a young Labrador called George, who was scarcely more than a puppy. All, however, were larger than Goofy; if one landed on him in rough and tumble, his back or hip could give way.

My arm was broken; the shoulder socket had

fractured vertically in three places. Unable to sleep, despite painkillers, I called from the hospital for bulletins. The first night, Goofy had stayed by the back entrance gate, waiting for me to come, until the kindness of Elvira persuaded him to come in for the night. Then, it was a lonely vigil by the door. A couple of nights later, he opted to sleep with the prettiest of the live-in maids ("more than I have managed to do", Mark observed dryly) and then finally mounted to the second floor to the master's magnificent bedroom, where he displaced George on the master's bed, to George's life-long resentment.

After nearly a fortnight, I could leave hospital; but I could not look after myself. Mark insisted I should come and stay with him until better – after all, he said, he didn't want to lose Goofy. The extent of the affection in which Goofy was held in the household was made clear when I arrived. Goofy was too small, or too wary, to jump through the unfamiliar flap in the door that had been arranged so that the dogs could go out to relieve themselves in the evenings, when their dog-walker had gone home. As the call of nature became more insistent, he – who never, ever soiled a house – must have looked desperately for a solution. Mark's bathroom of Carrara marble led into what had been described in design magazines as one of the most beautiful dressing rooms in the world. In exquisite hand-made wardrobes, bespoke shirts, Italian ties and beautiful suits were ranged immaculately. Goofy must have searched for somewhere unobtrusive;

finally he found it in a far corner closet. He had crapped inside one of Mark's hand-made Italian shoes. My cries of apology were waved aside. "Luckily", said Mark, "it was very firm."

The designer Jasper Conran has a slim, impossibly boyish physique; a loud, wicked laugh; and a very big heart. Seeing that it would be weeks before I could drive again, and that therefore I was stranded in London, he arranged grandly for his chauffeur to drive me down to my beloved cottage each weekend with Goofy. It was a tremendous kindness, and the dog adored it. As I tried to brace myself against the gentle swaying motion in the car – at that stage, while my shoulder and arm were mending without a plaster cast, the slightest shift could be agony – Goofy sat on my lap and wedged himself solidly between the two front seats, front paws on the Jaguar's central leather arm-rest. It was pole position and he knew it. He looked out, revelling in his elevation like the captain on the bridge, his head level with John the chauffeur's as we drove. Goofy looked carefully at everything that passed us by; when he caught sight of a large cat I felt an inner rumble.

John the driver became a friend. The atmosphere in the car was a happy one; it was the three of us – the oddest of trios – against the world. On the Sunday, John would collect us to do the return journey to London, and tell us all about his exploits in the merchant navy, as a butcher, and as a worry to his old Mum – whom he adored. All this high life in limousines gave Goofy such a passionate identification with Jaguars that, if we passed the Connaught hotel as the doorman was opening the door of one, some large American lady would get a lap-full of dog, as Goofy, presuming Jaguar doors were opened for him personally, leapt on top of her.

CHAPTER 10

Babe magnet

Goofy wasn't a clinging lapdog; he was a boisterous free spirit. But he seemed to worry what might happen to me, if he wasn't there to oversee things. As a result, I was the one on a short lead. It was true that I didn't go out as much, or venture as far: foreign travel lost its allure. Why bother, when we could go out, the two of us, and I could share the absolute joy of my dog, as he raced along the towpath by the river, fringed by fields, or sniffed his way along the hedgerows for partridges?

I could not have brought him to a better home. In green, rainy England, he was literally in his element. He would stare for hours at a patch of earth in the garden and then dart forward for bouts of furious digging, pulling out fibrous roots with his teeth until his entire body, ears and even eyelashes were coated in sticky mud.

He would ooze muddy satisfaction, as he extracted a nest of rabbits or baby rats. In the fields, one paw raised like a pointer, he would sniff the delicious coded wind.

He was a hunter. A real hunter. I had a personal, entirely unproven theory about this. In Greece, every small boy believes that manhood consists in possessing a gun to kill small birds in the winter; those unfortunate birds that could be trapped, had been hunted almost to extinction. All over Paxos one found piles of vainly spent cartridges. Whereas English shoots were organised formally, with beaters and dogs trained to retrieve what their masters shot, in the anarchic hunting of the Greek, many just shot what happened to pass by. I suspected that on Paxos, at least, they didn't hit much. Goofy had learned to supply their deficiency; he would find and kill a bird, and bring it back. He was so proud when he first brought supper for me that he seemed deeply disappointed by my reaction. On an estate with an expensive shoot, it was a disaster. A second time, when he had been unable to resist the instinct to kill, his expression was partly rebellious, partly submissive – like a naughty boy awaiting a punishment that, perhaps, had come all too savagely in the past.

For our walks around the estate, I found an immensely long extending lead: now, when something slaughtered their birds, the blame could never fall on Goofy. He ran free, however, along the lovely reaches of the Kennet and Avon canal, past locks and fields. One bright afternoon, I lost him: he had disappeared into a vast field of eye-smarting yellow oilseed rape. The stalks were stiff as broccoli, dense and almost immoveable. Whereas one could see Goofy making waves in a field of barley, now he was lost to view. Twenty minutes passed, despite my calls. Finally something crawled out fifty yards away. Those stalks had been full of sap . . . it was a sticky, bright green dog.

It was a process of mutual initiation. He learned to adapt into every aspect of my life; in turn I learned the extraordinary rigmarole of dog owning: tick removal; grooming; dietary needs; and cleaning up after him. It is just as well that the English are preoccupied with bowel movements. Every morning, one had to try not to lose one's breakfast while scooping up a smear of something unmentionable into a plastic bag. I had wondered if I would ever overcome my squeamishness; but within a month, I found a deep satisfaction in noting size, consistency, probable ingredients . . . it was fine, if it was from one's own dog. Some of those who came to know him felt the same; my secretary was especially sympathetic to all things Goofy. One day, I had flown to Salzburg for a meeting with the President and officers of the Festival, and my mobile phone bleeped, indicating a text message. "You have the information from your office?" they enquired, politely. It was from my assistant: GOOD WALK ONE BAG ALL NORMAL.

Gradually, Goofy ensured that our world contained

just two of us. Leaving him meant that wherever I went, I would see that little face, eyes fixed on the front door, not moving till I returned. So we were always, always together. Just as he came each day to my office, where he curled up beneath my desk, a soothing, loving presence, so in the country he regulated my day, punctuating it with walks, and pauses for affection. I walked around with a smile on my face, because people smiled when they saw him; we strutted along, each idiotically proud of the other. I avoided travel or late nights out; shopping was no longer a matter of browsing through boutiques – shopping was for essentials, like liver and pig's ears. There seemed nothing lonely about my cottage in the woods, up a rough track miles from a road, when there were two of us by the log fire, sharing roast chicken for supper. At night, the owls hooted, but I had the reassuring warmth of Goofy, curled up and dreaming of the day's rabbits, a tiny corner of pink tongue visible.

There was no escaping it: I was no longer inclined to be a party girl. Nor was I at the time in a relationship; if sometimes I woke at night alone, there was Goofy, as constant as grave goods, guarding me for the whole of his small eternity. As I looked at the dog curled on the bed beside me, a sleepy thought occurred: *perhaps the best man won . . .*

It was just as well. Goofy was not the dog to enjoy rivals for my affection. One crisp, early winter morning, we went into Grosvenor Square to fill the first bag of the morning. Seated on a bench reading a Herald Tribune in the pale early morning sun was a man in a rather good suit, with a briefcase – one of those fine old-fashioned leather satchels with flap and a lock. He smiled and struck up conversation. We talked politely for some time, and perhaps I should have noticed that Goofy was looking at us very closely. He watched the man ask me questions; he then looked at me for my reply. Finally, he walked stiffly and very deliberately over to the bench where the American, who had commented "Nice dog!" sat. Goofy gravely raised a hind leg – and peed all over the briefcase I had admired. After my initial shock, I registered the fact that the case was actually open, and all the papers inside were soaked. The nice American's tone became gutteral. "Don't you think you could teach your dog not to do that?" he growled. I stuttered an abject apology. Goofy had never done such a thing before. "I'm afraid I don't have anything to mop up with", I said. "But I live only round the corner; perhaps I could get a cloth and some disinfectant?" As if his limit of self-restraint had been reached, the American raised his hand: "*Just leave . . .*"

My brother, who was staying with me, was highly amused. "He doesn't do that when I take him out! It's completely the opposite. He goes straight for the prettiest girls, and he chats them up for us. He never fails", he said, in awed respect. "That dog is a *babe magnet . . .*"

CHAPTER 11

Everyday miracles

One morning when chasing after a ball, Goofy turned around suddenly, in the middle of Hyde Park, and stopped there. I heard a scream as I ran towards him. His body was locked in a circle upon itself, like a corkscrew. Gingerly I tried, as he cried out, to straighten him out, massaging and comforting him. He tried to go on – but after a few steps, it was agony. He just stood still, looking up at me. We were a long way from home, and from any transport. I picked him up – alas he was far too long a dog to be comfortable as I carried him; either the front or the back end would sink lower and drag on those painful ligaments. In the car, too, as I rushed him to the vet, I could hear that every jolt was agony.

It was typical of Goofy that he always had a disaster

out of hours, so that we had to go to a weekend, late-night or Bank holiday casualty place in Belgravia, rather than to reassuring Keith Butt, Goofy's vet in South Kensington, who knew his history encyclopaedically. At Elizabeth Street, inevitably road accident victims came first – and I became desperate, waiting with my suffering dog. We were loaded up with anti-inflammatories and pain killers, but on returning home Goofy couldn't rest. He seemed to need to keep moving, and throughout the night we padded the streets, while I pondered whether the pain of going down the stairs to get out, did more harm than the relief of walking.

The surgeon we consulted said that a metal plate could be welded between the shoulder and the wasted leg. But Goofy only had intermittent spells of incapacity and it appeared his spine was fractured long ago; adding the extra weight of a metal plate could be counter-pro-ductive. Goofy had gradually taught his body to compensate; yet the more he favoured his strong leg, to spare the pain, the more distorted his body became. It was literally a vicious circle. It was now necessary to watch Goofy very closely when we were running around together. If his back leg began to drag, that was the hint to stop before he did himself a major injury. Suddenly I had a medical excuse for becoming what originally I had most abhorred: the over-anxious pet owner.

In the course of some work with medical charities, I met a number of highly-qualified doctors who were in favour of complementary medicine. I had developed a great respect for the osteopaths and acupuncturists amongst them. Would it work on dogs? Every Wednesday, the Bayswater Referral Clinic hosted a highly qualified conventional vet who had turned to acupuncture and homeopathy. I asked my vet Keith Butt – who agreed that Richard Allport was the man to try.

This tiny piece of Bayswater was a sunny place. The dogs and cats in the waiting room were relatively unstressed; but Goofy was wary enough to practice his favourite trick in vet's waiting rooms – that of refusing to sit on the floor beside my legs. He insisted on sitting on a chair beside me, so that when his name was called, he would loftily ignore it. *Me? I'm not a patient.* After a dog or cat was taken into the consulting room, one could hear no yelps, no scuffles, no howls. When the door opened, the beaming faces of the owners spoke volumes.

Richard Allport had a modest, kind, quietly humorous face; at the first appointment he took Goofy's history in such minute, caring detail that I felt jealous of the dog. This, I thought, is the sort of NHS care that would be provided in heaven. He felt Goofy's sore joints with a gentle grace, apologising to him in a comforting way when the dog registered discomfort. Next, needles. To my surprise, Goofy winced but did not try to scrabble to remove them; after twenty seconds, his eyes began somehow to lose focus – he looked woozy, as if he were falling asleep. "Some patients actually do", said Richard.

Despite all those needles, Goofy never once bit Richard. He was a perfect miracle of ambivalence, charging into Richard's room, giving him such a big hello that love was not a too strong a word for his feelings – tempered, once he'd licked him hello, with wariness: after all, a vet was a vet. Goofy would then retreat under the chair I sat on, doleful eyes peering out between my legs. I would rise and Richard would quietly lift the chair away, leaving an exposed Goofy who would sigh, as if resigned to something that he knew would do him good. And what good it was: within three weeks, my agonised, crippled dog was almost off anti-inflammatory tablets and pain killers; after six, he was climbing stairs again and jumping. Acupuncture attracts bitter sceptics; but Goofy was not on any other treatment to which his improvement could be attributed; his diminished pain meant that I gave him more exercise, with more likelihood of injury, than formerly; and it couldn't be a placebo. After all, no one had told Goofy that his treatment was the result of 3,000 years of Chinese medicine.

CHAPTER 12

Bravado

One grey January day, Goofy fell ill with a set of symptoms I had never seen before. He was hunched over with pain; he couldn't eat and he was very cold. At the vets' hospital in the country, they were perplexed; they put him on painkillers and heavy antibiotics and said I could take him home next morning – where he promptly collapsed. Back in hospital, he went on a drip; a sorry figure shivering in a little cage. When he saw me, he would make a magnificent effort at a welcome. Then followed long days and nights of waiting for test results, my heart thudding in staccato jumps of anxiety as I made calls each day, for results that might spell tragedy, as he became both swollen with fluid and emaciated.

It is difficult for dogs to communicate with us. That they try so hard to do so is all the more significant. Many times Goofy had shown a tenderness when a small child teased him and pulled his ears, that showed an enviable strength of will. Now he was concentrating the whole of his small being into coming home. I would visit him in hospital, holding back tears in the car park at the heart-rending sight of his struggle to come back to me. They couldn't identify the cause of problem; one young vet mentioned "letting him go". Keith Butt, my London vet, saw the notes from the country and rang with concern, comfort and advice.

When, after two weeks in the country hospital, he had swollen horrendously with fluid, they said I should drive him to a referral clinic hospital, over a hundred miles away in Hertfordshire. I was glad there was action; but what would I do if Goofy went into a crisis while we were alone on the motorway?

I don't know what I would have done without my dear friend Jan; he came up to the cottage and rose at 5 am to help me by driving my car, as I map-read and we tried to second-guess the traffic hold-ups. There was only one precious 9.30 am slot for an appointment with a specialist, and if we didn't make it . . .

We found the referral clinic; it was a modern complex that had clustered, like a group of grey limpets, in the middle of bleak and windswept fields. Shivering, we carried Goofy in through the sleet which raked a clutch of low buildings. In the reception area, all seemed reassuringly professional.

The specialist came down a corridor at 9.30 exactly. I thought of *House*, the TV series about a brilliant diagnostic doctor who specialises in solving medical mysteries; here was a fitter, more approachable House, for dogs. For the first time I felt a lift of hope; I was treated as an intelligent individual not an hysterical pet-owner, though, exhausted as I was, he could have been forgiven for seeing me as the latter. I was given real hard information: unfortunately it was very real and very hard indeed.

I found somewhere to stay nearby for days; if the outcome was bad, I didn't want Goofy to die without me. Goofy bore with kidney section and lumbar puncture and I got to know about obscure diseases, as they struggled, so late in the day, for a diagnosis; I learnt words like glomerulonephtritis and amyloidosis and of course I scoured the internet. There I saw the bare words *Prognosis: very poor.*

The doctor, Clive Elwood, was marvellous: incisive, direct and thorough. I asked him to tell me if I was being foolish – or selfish – in keeping him alive. He said he felt that the dog hadn't given up, so we shouldn't. But there was serious kidney damage; in quiet straightforward words he prepared me for the emaciated and weak dog I was to take home, and said he might have weeks, not months. I said I understood; I did not. Clive warned that sometimes dogs in the final stages of this condition went into acute distress and could die suddenly; he described how one of his patients had undergone what he referred to as a "catastrophic event".

The dog who came out was shocking. His suffering had etched itself on his face; his testes, swollen and cracked, gave him acute discomfort; they had put a hard Elizabethan collar on him to prevent him licking off sore skin. He was skeletally thin.

But from the minute I got him home, Goofy fought for life. In the long nights he could not rest easily, and every groan or turn made me anxious. If he was restive I got up to soothe him; if silent and still, to check if he were still alive. I nursed him right through each night, both of us near exhaustion; and with heart-rending effort, he came back to me. Soon he wanted walks in the fields; he dug a delightfully muddy hole in the garden; he got out favourite toys, and he regained weight. I began to nurse wild fancies that he would beat the odds. I wrote reports back to the specialist: *I said heart-broken farewells to Goofy in the early hours of yesterday morning, as he was in a sad state – but all through the night, despite problems, he hung on. This morning, he felt like breakfast; spat out his tablets with the old vigour; and on his morning walk he pursued a spaniel bitch on heat . . . He has diarrhoea, but no discomfort; and his eyes are brighter. We went to Richard Allport, who was very complimentary about all you'd done, and said that considering everything, the emaciation and frailty weren't as bad as he had feared. Goofy has now kept down two days' worth of meals (served in small snacks to avoid nausea) and I've got some soothing calendula lotion to sort out the sore swollen*

testes, which has added much to canine contentment! Still, after two
exhausting nights of thinking that he wasn't going to make it, the
little b****** is now begging for treats. A very short-lived break
from what is to come, I know, but I somehow feel that it justifies all
the intervention.

Clive Elwood replied comfortingly that we should see
what his blood tests looked like at the end of the week –
and told us to hang on in there . . .

By the end of that week, Goofy had once again risen
above his fate; he had gained more weight; he managed
almost an unbroken night of sleep – and I lapsed into
short bursts of exhausted rest. Rationally, I told myself
that shortly he would die. Emotionally, I could not comprehend it. What kept me going during the following
days was that he was not left in distress and loneliness
away from me in the veterinary hospital; he knew I had
not abandoned him to his fate. He was home: we could
put the tubes, the biopsies, the lumbar punctures, and all
the strange and distressing impersonality of hospital
behind us.

Then for a few days he started to be unable to keep food
down and I trembled. Surely not . . . I took him back to
the country hospital, where mercifully the senior vet was
on duty. Goofy was bright and alert, he agreed, and said
he didn't think it was time for euthanasia; he'd keep him
in for injections and tests – I could return at midday.
Exhausted and now permanently fearing the worst, I

wandered aimlessly from shop to shop, where the shop-keepers were Goofy's friends; from his first arrival in England, the Hungerford bookshop had kept a special bowl for him. To my surprise the news at midday was reassuring; I could come back at six and take him home.

But at six, the vet had further news. "I'm afraid I was misled in my first diagnosis because Goofy is trying to pretend he's all right, in order to come home to you. It's bravado. He is much sicker than we originally thought. You asked if it was time . . . I think, now, it is". Part of me wanted to rush through the hospital and grab my little boy (because he was my little boy) and run away. But I thought about that "catastrophic event". It should not be Goofy's catastrophic event. It should be mine . . . Somehow with the vet's support I found the courage for my decision.

I will never, ever forget the next twenty minutes, as I prepared to kill the dog who loved me. Goofy pushed out of his pen when he saw me, nosing at the door for us to leave. He was given a sedative injection, and I was told to my horror that I could walk him round outside for several minutes, while it took effect. Outside, Goofy saw the car, and tried weakly to go towards it . . . *Mummy, let's go home.*

When he looked at me aghast, no longer able to move, I carried him into the hospital to the bare operating table.

I wish I could say what followed was dignified, or beautiful. There, while he was still conscious, I had to hold him tightly, too tightly, as the lethal injection finally turned him into something very different and alien. The vet's eyes too were a little wet: perhaps because this is an area of unsung heroism in vets; perhaps he saw the very moment my heart broke.

CHAPTER 13

Now he is gone

Now he is gone, and his absence is everywhere. Clutching an empty collar, I drove home alone for the first time in ten years, and as I bumped over the track to the cottage, no furry face would ever again pop up in the driving mirror, excited at homecoming. Indoors, never again would I hear a bump, bump, as he made his way downstairs in the mornings, to ask for the hairdryer to warm his sore shoulder. The patch on the bed which he had made his own; the countless moments each day when I would feel a lick of my hand, or the pressure of a paw. After his death, I would wake up and find myself standing alone on the bedroom floor at four in the morning, still checking in my sleep on a dog who was lost forever.

Walks in the fields and woods round the cottage

became painful and somehow pointless. Every path was familiar; but it led only to where he was not. People may say he was only a dog; that I allowed him to mean far, far too much. But our deepest communication is without words; and what Goofy gave me was a canine lesson in love: utterly single-minded, total devotion. He gave me his whole heart; so I simply did the same. A silent bond of immense tenderness has been broken. Losing him has meant bereavement of such depth that it has astonished and marked me: I had not thought such sorrow lay at the heart of all this love. It has cost cold days and nights of grief – and, my Goofy, I wouldn't have missed a minute of them.

In the days that followed, I kept seeing again the moment of his death; as I stroked him, numb with grief, a young vet who had seen Goofy when he first fell ill, passed by the operating table where Goofy lay. Perhaps out of awkwardness, he flicked his fur with a finger and thumb and passed on. It was not an action he would have done to a living animal; and in that one gesture, the identity of the dog I loved was destroyed. I felt something inside me – that wave of absurd, irrational hope that that it wasn't really happening – ebb and drain out of me.

After his death, people looked suddenly upset when they greeted me in the street, having searched round and behind me in vain for my shadow: the dog who had so endeared himself to them. Many people wrote me letters:

a widow wrote that her husband had died, leaving her alone but for a dog who meant everything to her. Whose loss, she said, was unbearable and lonely in a way that, God forgive her, the loss of her husband had not been. I felt, too, that Goofy was a finger in the dyke, holding back a sea of troubles and unhappiness. Now he had gone, dark waters flowed in . . .

All broken. All gone. Why should the loss of a pet affect us so? I think that just as the losses in an earthquake, or war, are too big for us to comprehend, so this small finality of death is on a scale that we can feel truthfully. Like Goldilocks in the home of the three bears, we find that there is one sorrow, one bed, that is exactly the right size for us. When we lie upon it, it fills us exactly . . . with its emptiness.

It is odd what you can learn from a small stray dog's devotion. Goofy showed me that it is being able to *give* love that we crave. A dog rejoices in this communion: there is no cold shoulder; no shrinking from our touch. We are spared the hurt from the lover who turns away with a shrug; the child who suddenly grows up, and pushes away our arms.

I remember when my mother's mother died. I rang my mother to suggest that I could drive straight down to her; I could be at my parents' house in Devon within five hours. "Oh darling, that's very kind of you," she said: "But I think I'll be all right. The thing is, when the dog died four weeks ago, I think I cried myself out . . ." Like many things my mother says, this is both hilarious and true. Our griefs are not mutually exclusive. She mourned her mother deeply and sincerely; but the death of a dog cuts open a vein: we bleed. We have little idea of how to staunch it, without the props and comforts, the mourning rituals and beliefs that may support us in human bereavement.

In the months following Goofy's death, I wondered whether there was something wrong with the profound way I mourned him. But the pity of it would not be denied. This is not weakness: it is a due repaid to one who had greatness of heart. Since Goofy died, I have heard of one of the hardest, toughest of men, who wept inconsolably when his own small dog was killed in an accident. So we are not that tough. Why do we weep such tears?

Probably, if we asked, dogs could tell us.

Useful Addresses

Dogs Trust
Foremost dog charity with regional re-homing centres
17 Wakley Street
London
EC1V 7RZ
020 7837 0006 (9am-5pm, Mon-Fri)
www.dogstrust.org.uk

Passports for Pets
Flat 11, 45 Queen's Gate
London
SW7 SHR
Tel. 020 7589 6404
Fax. 020 7589 6403

Rescue Dogs
A list of dogs in need of homes: www.rescue-dogs.co.uk

The Pet Bereavement Support Service
Helpline 8.30am-8.30pm 0800 096 6606
Run by the Blue Cross www.bluecross.org.uk

Cinnamon Trust
A charity devoted to caring for animals when their owner
has died.
10 Market Square
Hayle
Cornwall
TR27 4HE
01736 757900

Animal Rescue Charity
Foxdells Lane
Rye Street
Bishops Stortford
Herts
CM23 2JG
www.animalrescue.org.uk
email: support@animalrescue.org.uk
Tel. 0870 770 2660

The Pets Travel Scheme

Government regulations on pet travel: www.defra.gov.uk

It is important to note that there are changes to approved routes, carriers and regulations governing admittance from different countries, so one must check the Defra website.

The UK PETS scheme currently applies in the following countries only: Andorra, Austria, Belgium, Denmark, Finland, France, Germany, Gibraltar, Greece, Iceland, Italy, Liechtenstein, Luxembourg, Monaco, The Netherlands, Norway, Portugal, San Marino, Spain, Sweden, Switzerland and the Vatican.

You must have a vet's certificate to show that your pet is fitted with a microchip, vaccinated against rabies, and successfully blood tested. You must also have an official PES certificate. You will have to wait at least 6 months (the time it takes for the rabies virus to become apparent and to ensure they did not contract the disease before inoculation).WARNING - many attempts to get cats and dogs into the UK fail due to incorrect documentation.

Information on DEFRA PETS HELPLINE 0870 241 1710 (8.30am - 5.00pm Monday to Friday) – leave your name and address for a information pack. Be prepared to wait - they do not answer promptly! Fax: 020 7904 6834. Or write to: Export of Cats and Dogs Section, DEFRA, 1A Page Street, London SW1P 4PQ. Factsheets – online or download a PDF sheet. www.defra.gov.uk/animalh